I Can Be Pretty

By Edward Holmes

ACCLIVITY PUBLISHING

To request permissions, contact the publisher at AcclivityPublishing@gmail.com

Hardcover: 978-0-578-31633-8

Illustration and Cover art by Tais Lemos

Printed in the USA

For Jaeda...

You're pretty amazing.

What if my hair is an ocean of curls that
entangle my ears with a million swirls?

Would I be pretty with straight hair that flows
like a river of gold from my head to my toes?

What if I have to wear glasses or braces
and freckles are found on the flanks of my face?

Would I be pretty with pearly white teeth
and I never had freckles that speckle my cheeks?

What if I'm having some
trouble with height
and I feel my
complexion just isn't
quite right?

Would I be pretty if I were much taller
than short and had skin with a little more color?

What if my clothes aren't the popular type and I'd rather wear hoodies that snuggle just right?

Would I be pretty if all that I wore
was trendy and cost just a little bit more?

All of these questions are swirling about
and they're starting to fill up
my headspace with doubt .

But I think that I finally figured it out
and I've come to conclude that it's not all about...

Every shoe that I wear,

or the style of my hair,

or the skin that I'm in,

If I'm fuller or thin.
I've been created to do
so much more
So if I can be pretty,
then one thing's for
sure...

I can be pretty
intelligent.

Physical qualities?
Fairly irrelevant.
Knowledge is power,
and I've got a lot.

I'll change the world with
the *wisdom* I've got.

I can be pretty
creative,
using my talents to be
innovative.

Starting a business and
leading a team
is possible when I hold
fast to my dream!

I can be pretty *compassionate*.

Helping out others is easy when tasked with a problem too heavy for them to withstand.

I can give back to the world through my hands.

I can be pretty
inspiring,
using encouraging words,
never tiring of speaking
life into hearts that are sore.

I can speak life
as an author or more!

I can be pretty *benevolent*.

Helping out those who are hurting is simple when we take a step with the smallest of deeds by *giving* to those with the greatest of needs.

Girls can be anything they want to be.
More than a face in a mirror, you see.
More than an image, or swipe on a screen,
but brimming inside with the wildest of dreams.

So, If I'm pretty,
I'm pretty incredible, capable, powerful,
never forgettable.

Positive, brave and uniquely designed
with a purpose with worth more than
rubies, you'll find.

I'm woven together with threads of
adventure deep down in my center
and brimming with splendor.

I'm capable, limitless, strong,
and resilient. Perfectly made and
incredibly brilliant.

Charm is deceptive,
and beauty is fleeting
so, modifications are not
what I'm needing.

So I'll never worry if "I measure up,"
for I'm pretty sure...

I'll be more

than enough!

www.ingramcontent.com/pod-product-compliance
Ingram Content Group UK Ltd.
Pitfield, Milton Keynes, MK11 3LW, UK
UKHW061033310726
14089UKWH00010B/224
9780578316338